Random Musings of a Teenager... and Beyond

To every angst-riddled teen who grew up to be an angst-riddled adult...

CONTENTS

Forward

So, the innermost thoughts of a teenager are typically not for the faint of heart. There is nothing more dramatic on the planet, nothing more emotionally draining than going through one's teenage years. The mixture of no longer 'being a kid' and 'not quite an adult' is the most trying times of life.

Contained within the following pages are the random musings as collected in various Composition Books and journals dating back to age 15. Apparently for me, age 15 hit hard. Some of these writings have never seen the light of day while others have been either shared as homework assignments or entered into one of the many poetry contests I entered as a teenager. I've transcribed them as found, so no editing was done other than spelling errors and fixing a wayward comma or two, you know, to preserve the angst. In reviewing some of these stories and poetic contemplations, it is amazing I survived!

Random Musings

Emotions

I keep my emotions bottled up in a bottle,

So if I ever feel like I am lost on a beach,

I have something to throw into the ocean,

So somebody knows where I could be reached.

Age 15

Random Musings

My Outlook of My Life (figuratively)

Once I was

A set of oil paints

Alone on a palette

Now I am

Part of an artist's painting

Being looked at with judgement.

Age 15

Random Musings

Childhood Memories

Childhood is walking up early on Christmas morning.

Childhood is wide-eyed innocence and not-me's when your mother asks who broke the dish.

Childhood is playing tang and hide and go seek with the other kids.

Childhood is never getting tired of the swings in the park.

Childhood is having bike races around the street.

Childhood is roller skates and roller rinks.

Childhood is birthday parties with ice cream cake and pin-the-tail-on-the-donkey.

Childhood is forever.

Age 15

Random Musings

Love is Just

Love is just another four-letter word.

Some men seek it, other dare not speak it, and yet others can, and probably have been broken by it.

Love is just another element that everyone has to deal with.

Love has it emotions too…it may frown upon you or grace you with its presence. It could be sneaky and surprise you.

Love is just another four-letter word.

Love is just another element.

Love is just…

Age 15

Random Musings

Is he the one?

There was a point in time,

Many years ago,

That there was a possible answer,

By now I do not know.

We were a 'couple'

But it was only for a time.

There really as a period

That I was his and he was mine.

We went our separate ways,

And for a time that seemed like forever, I was sad,

When I released he was gone,

And I remembered the fun we had.

But he may be coming back,

And we might have our time in the sun.

So now I face this questions again:

Is he the one?

Age 15

Random Musings

The Feared Place

White wall surround, enclose.

Carts with screeching wheels pass by the door, collecting uneaten meals, and continue down the hall.

People in white – everywhere. Everything coated in the placid color.

This place, where death doth seem to linger, many fear, despise, with just cause. Although this place may help, save, it, all at the same time, can take away.

Age 15

Random Musings

They Danced

They met at the dance. At first, they stared at each other, secret glances, sly, undetected glances, hoping the other would not catch them in the act. Then finally he walked to her and handsomely asked her to dance. And they walked towards the dance floor. He put his arms around her – she quivered. He wanted to say something. He tried to say something, but he faltered. So they danced. Not much was said – not much was needed to be said. What they wanted to say seemed to be said by their eyes, which both stared into the others, which seemed like an eternity. The he drew her closer to him, embracing her, holding her there, in his arms, dancing, shutting his eyes – he, nor she, did not want the song to end. Both danced, each embracing the other, eyes shut, each trying to make the moment last. The song, which played for a long time, which seemed like forever, came to its end, and yet, even though it had ended, they danced...

Age 16

Random Musings

How did he know?

How did he know? I just wonder. I did not tell him. Sure I had plenty of chances. I was even planning on telling him, but then I found out that he already knew! No one else told him because they knew that I wanted to tell him myself. Doesn't he know how long it took me to find the words to tell him? How much courage it took me to even approach him or to approach the subject? But I never got the chance. He already knew, but how? No one told. Did I give out any signals? Any looks? How did he know?

Age 16

Random Musings

How long do I have to wait?

How long do I have to wait,

For me to know

In which direction

That I should go?

Should I follow my heart

To where it may take me;

Or to follow the voice of reason,

But that path I wish not see.

For that path

Does not comply

With the path my heart

Tells me to try.

Age 16

Random Musings

A Questioning Soul

Why must life be a mystery?

Why isn't there some sort of passage for souls to follow?

Why must everything be a memory?

Where are memories forgotten?

Where is the sense in forgetting something which was meant to be remembered?

How come we can never remember that moment where we fall in love, but we can always remember the moment when we lost it?

What is the true purpose of crying?

What exactly is a good cry when on cries out of remorse, regret, or sadness?

Where is the rhythm in the rhyme, the method in the maddens, the logic in my world of confusion?

Why must there be so many questions without answers?

Why?

Age 17

Random Musings

Creatures I have encountered

The glowing sphere sinks into the distance. It is not envious of her nocturnal sister, her pale while sister which bring out the creatures. They only appear at night with their eyes, piercing the dark. Two types appear; the ones with the bright white eyes and then there are the others, the ones with eyes so red they scream evil. The latter are most confusing to me for they are always facing me, but they tend to travel backwards as if they are following my movements as I follow them. I always seem to be behind these red-eyed devils. After a brief game of follow-the-leader, this creature increases his pace as if to suggest perhaps to either get away from me or maybe, just maybe, it wishes to see if my curiosity will bet the best of me and chase him.

As we approach the hill, I could see him rise with the train and disappear as if swallowed by the night. As my fiendish friend vanishes another creature arise from the other side, an even exchange. This creature is of

the white, bright eyed persuasion. It's eyes almost blind me for I was not prepared for the brightness being accustomed to the dull glow of the red eyes. The while eyes pass me, a refreshing change on this lonely path. As I cleared the hill, I catch the glimpse of the red eyes once again. This time I am determined to catch up to this creature to make out just what this thing is. Closer and closer I get until I am maybe only a couple of yards away. I can just make out some sort of markings above one of his eyes. Yes, I can see it clearly now. Perhaps it is a name? The name of the creature I have chase so diligently is Volvo.

Age 17

Random Musings

At Night's End

As the gold drenched orb ascends into the waterless blue ocean, thoughts gather as if gale winds sweep those forgotten ornaments, that have fallen from wooden plants. Hazy images at first, but as dawn is eminent, the stronger images appear like those of angel's dreams, children's laughter, happier cays when fear was by only rumor. Those days long past, stored away, placed ever so carefully in trunks that have been hidden from view. Obscure images come and go playing crew tricks to a tired, weary soul. A soul that has almost forgotten what it is to laugh.

Age 18

Random Musings

Plagiarism of Emotions

Did you say you love me because I said if first?

Are you going through the motions for my sake or for yours?

What are your true feelings or do you even know yourself?

How am I to know what direction to go when I am depending on you to show me the way?

Do you know the less I get from you, the less I get to give to you?

Should I demand answers to my mounting questions or should I wait for you to demand yourself to answer your own questions?

And if I choose to wait, will I be waiting forever?

Age 17

Random Musings

He and She

She sat beside him under the old oak tree.

He, not knowing what she was thinking.

She not knowing his thoughts at all.

He is very timid.

She as well, or maybe even more so.

He was wondering if he should make the first move.

She was wondering the same.

He, trying to build up the courage to attempt a conversation.

She mustering up some strength to utter some words.

He made the attempted but faltered.

She nodded nervously in response.

He returned to their silent state, the same as before,

She sat beside him under the old oak tree.

Age 18

Random Musings

Expecting the Unexpected

The light from my lantern casts an eerie glow upon the walls of the cavern. The only sound is that which the cavern's floor makes with each step I take. That sickening slush of mud against the weight of my body echoes down this darkened corridor. As I approach the turn, the shadows grow; I creep cautiously in fear of what lies ahead around the bend. My imagination runs wild as the light dances upon the mis-sharpened wall and creates fictious creatures lurking ahead of me. I near the corner, my heart pounding, beads of sweat form along my brow, my breathing becomes more and more difficult as I proceed, as if my own fear is strangling me. I feel constricted as I round the corner and the fear that almost paralyzed me dissipates, for all that is there is a continuation of this bleak corridor, with what seems to have no end.

Age 18

Random Musings

Terror in Progress

She fumbled around in the dark in search for a candle or better yet, something she could use for defense. Whoever it was outside found his way to the power box and to the telephone line and made sure both were damaged beyond repair. She continued to scamper around in desperation. Terrified, trembling, and fearful for her safety, she gives up the search and figures it better if she just finds a safe spot to hide. Crouched in the crawlspace, she listens intensely for the man who has been stalking her.

He finally gets fed up with the taunting her and wants in. The soon to be intruder grabbed a large rock from the garden outside and smashes the living room's picture window. He climbs into the house cautiously. The only light that pierces the darkened house is the glow from the full moon. She peers out of her hiding spot long enough to see the moonlight reflecting off his knife. The hunt begins...

Age 18

Random Musings

The Imaginary Tree

It's not there.

The poor acorn I nursed to a sapling is no longer there.

What happened?

I remember being so proud that I was able to coax a small, limp sapling from that acorn.

I even remember planting it in the back yard.

I nurtured it to be, I thought, a strong young tree.

The day came when we had to move. I so upset. I had to leave my young dependent behind.

Upset that I could not see that tree grow to adulthood.

My only recourse was to imagine it grow big and strong and was the most gorgeous tree even saw.

Recently I had the chance to visit my tree.

It's not there.

Someone said it died after I left.

I often wonder, was it from loneliness that it died, or was I not the gardener I thought I was?

Age 19

Random Musings

Advice

Don't think.

Feel.

Let it flow; not just form you, but through you.

If you push too had for images, you will only get he same old tired one as before.

Don't worry about subject, content.

None of that truly matters.

Just write.

Don't analyze your surroundings for an item in which to write about.

The last thing you should be concerned about is a strong finish (especially if you have yet to begin!)

Don't fret over what to write next.

Don't think...

Don't worry...

Don't analyze...

Don't fret...

Feel...

Age 19

Random Musings

Was it the wrong thing to do?

Clatter, smash, boom!

An unanticipated crash shakes me and knocks me to the ground.

Gravity once again rules.

I clear the debris from my now bruised body and try to regain my composure.

What a mess.

Everything is scattered everywhere.

It looks as if a hurricane passed through this way,

When all I did was open my closet door.

Age 19

Random Musings

Clueless

Walking through a mystery.

A mystery which drapes around me like a thick moist fog.

Unsure in which direction I am going.

Lost, and no clue to govern me.

Images are hazy and nothing is clear to me anymore.

The only sounds I hear is that of the slosh my footsteps make on this maddened path; accompanied by that of lowly crickets and air occasional owl.

I feel I have been led astray by those who brought me here.

I look for those "faithful" companions and find they are gone.

Did I lose them somewhere along this path or have they decided to leave me and mean for me to go on alone?

Age 19

Random Musings

Chase in Progress

She trips over a tuff of grass and falls. Struggling to conquer gravity, she slips on the wet, slick grass once again. Finally she is able to achieve some sort of traction and pushes off of the ground with her hands and runs up the remaining small hill. Her pursuer gained some ground during her bout with gravity. He is close enough to gab the sleeve of her while sweater. Once he thinks he has a firm hold of her, he attempts to move in on his prey. However, she is able to shake her attacker by coaxing her way out of her once buttoned up sweater. In the process of escaping his near grip, she was practically spun around and almost lost yet another battle with gravity. She does break away and heads towards what she thinks will be her salvation, a patch of trees. Perhaps, she thinks, she can lose him within their shelter. As she entered the miniature forest, she immediately looked for a spot to hide. While running she momentarily glanced up to see the full moon seemingly dance amongst the tree limbs.

She no longer heard her would be attacker behind her and threw a glance over her shoulder to see whether or not he was there. She did not see him and briefly was relieved; however, she wondered where he was. She got her answer for after she flipped her head around, she realized he was right in front of her, and she unknowingly ran smack into his awaiting arms...

Age 19

Random Musings

Stalking in Progress

She is eloquently dressed. Hair done right, sleek black velvet dress. Un aware that as she exist the theatre she is being watched like a hawk observes its prey. She tried to hail a cab, but the all elude her. She decides to walked some, all the while persistent on trying to obtain a cab. All the while being followed. He stays a good distance behind, but close enough to grab her at any moment. As she walk, the only sound she hears is the hollow echo her stiletto heels make along the now empty streets. She notices how the shadows ris and fall as she passes. The darkened surroundings becoming more and more frightening as they are partially illuminated from the full moon above. She also noticed how her footstep seem to becoming louder. She doesn't quite understand until her heel snags a crack in the concrete and her patter is broke, but there still there is an echo of a footstep she did not take. She realized she is being followed. Quickly, threw a sharp look over her shoulder, scanning the darkness to see if

she can make out a figure when she suddenly notices him, the she notices the thin metallic wire he is holding. A wire meant for her perhaps? She breaks into a trot; her dress was not intended for running. He, knowing she cannot get far, toys with her, purposely staying behind, tormenting her. She is relieved in knowing the fact that she is only a few moments from home, from being safe. Finally she is able to see her home. He, for his own personal kicks, lets her think she is going to make it to her destination. She makes it to the gate, which for some reason gave her trouble this night, but with that finally opened, she fumbles with her purse to find her keys. She finds the right key and manages to get it in the lock and as she turns the key she looks straight ahead and notices how the moonlight reflects off the thin metal wire...

Age 19

Random Musings

Tournament in Progress

She walks to her mailbox, suspecting nothing. Inside was a manilla envelope with no return address. Curiously she examines the piece of amil as she walk s bac up the drive. She enters her kitchen and places the other mail on the table. Her curiosity is up and cannot stand to wait any longer. She opens the envelop to find a simple message: "I've been watching you." Simply scary. She gets the sudden feeling of paranoia. She becomes fearful of everything. Day by day, another envelope. She hates to open them but feels she must. She must know what he is going. All the messages ever said were the same as the first, except for this last one. The last anything she would ever receive, read a simple message: "Now I'm coming for you." She no longer went to for the mail. She no longer went outside. She slept very little, if at all at night. Almost a week or so go by and there is no sign of him. It was almost the third week after the last notice. It was 3 am and the moon was full. Surprisingly enough it was one of the nights

she was able to find sleep. She was awakened by what she thought was just a stray cat jumping on the metal garbage can outside her bedroom window. She couldn't be more wrong. She said up in her bend, put her face in her hands, gave a small huff, and decided to get up for a glass of water. As she placed her feet on the floor she looked up at the window. There he was! He looked at the now startled woman and he simply said: "I've been watching you."

Age 19

Random Musings

Cracks in the concrete

Sprouting from nowhere

Not ending, just disappointing

Crooked, uneven,

branching in all directions

Loners, pioneers,

scavengers in their own right

Searching out amongst new territory

Breaking the ground

Breaking the rules

Age 19

Random Musings

The Day I Realized Grover was Blind

My ragged old pal sits slumped at the head of my bed.

The stuffing that once supported his head had been loved away over the years.

His blue fur no longer sports the same luster I once did when he was new.

At times of loneliness he was there.

I would burl up with my blue buddy and confide my feelings to him.

After a while I dubbed him my crying buddy for every time I found myself crying, I found him in my arms.

One day, back in my childhood years, while replacing my pal back on his pillow throne, I observed

a change in him; that was the day; the day I realized Grover was blind.

His plastic painted peepers no longer had pupils.

The black painted circles rubbed off some from his plastic white eyes.

I took it upon myself to return 'sight' to him.

I obtained black paint and painted his new orbs of 'sight'.

To this day I do not understand why I found it an urgency to restore Grover's eyes.

Even at this 'advanced' age I am now, 19, I look over at my now traveling buddy and feel better knowing he's looking back.

Age 19

Random Musings

Description of an Unrequited Love

If a thrill can be obtained in a minute, he would be an hour.

I privately revel in his presence.

He has become my muse, my inspiration of occasional writing.

The most expressive of words could not begin to summarize emotions yet to be expressed; however.

It was the proverbial fireworks display I experienced when we first met.

I felt giddy and light-headed and felt perhaps I was not able to converse in any intelligible fashion.

The time flew.

Kathleen Lopez

Darkness full upon us and I was so enraptured with his now only semi-stranger, that I never paid notice to the absence of sunlight.

Since I met him, I haven't really noticed that months as well have gone by.

Time flies when you're occupied...

Age 19

Random Musings

Selecting a Reality

Through darkened clouds and hopeless nights, he arrived.

No fancy entrance, no warning given.

I reached out and found him there with open arms.

Suddenly I was not alone, but with a friend.

Time passed and our friendship grew.

In my mind was the foundation of a great love.

In secret I dedicated to him each victory.

I called to him in each defeat.

I prayed he felt the same.

I found myself falling in love with the idea of us.

Always fearing he considered us only friends.

I kept these feelings hidden, fearful of losing my friend.

Pent up emotions had started to get the best of me.

Images of him crept into my every thought.

Finally I had to confess.

The control that I had begun to fail me.

The moment had arrived for my confessional.

I attempted to speak but failed.

He grasped my hands, gazed into my eyes, eased my apprehensions.

I sense he knew and felt the same.

Perhaps.

Once my feats clamed, I spoke.

Spoke of emotions that were hidden by time, or by me.

A deep cleansing breath finished the speech and the door was finally unlocked.

Unsure that I should, not knowing what I would find, I slowly raised my eyes and met his.

My soul was lost within the icy blue tone.

At the moment for him to reply, as he opened his mouth to speak, I...woke.

Age 19

Random Musings

Stage Right

I have always thought I had things all planned out.

I knew all my entrances and exits.

My lines memorized; my character developed.

Suddenly the part I was playing changed.

A new character entered that I was not prepared for.

Now I have forgotten my lines; my character became foreign, even to me.

This character seems to have no rhyme nor reason.

One moment he is there, dependable, tangible,

The next he is gone.

To attempt to follow the script seems incredibly useless and futile.

I try to explain this character to myself,

Kathleen Lopez

Sometimes I even try to forget him,

But just as I try to erase him from my memory, he enters again, stage right.

Age 20

Random Musings

Measuring Up

There is this image of myself

I hold in my head.

You have no idea how I wish I was her.

There is no meaning or room for the word cautious to her.

She is danger, truth, honesty.

She creates her life while I try to color within the lines.

She always has the winning hand while I race to play 52 pickup.

She is the life of the party while my phone has dust on it.

The man in her life would die for her; I'm too afraid to ask who pays for dinner.

People around me hold the same image of me as the one I wish to be.

Kathleen Lopez

How I wish they were right!

Age 21

Random Musings

Punch Lady

I am the woman who hands out the punch at the party. I watch every dance; laughing couples twirling by while I dole out refreshments. Murmurs of conversations drift my way. "Can I have some punch please?" is the in-depth conversation I engage in. as if I had this power, to grant them permission. What else am I here for? Why else am I here?

I don't want my station behind the card table. I want to dance, converse, laugh. Instead, I am stuck behind this table. God forbid I do what I wish, though. It always seems that people look to me to be the planner, the one who makes sure things like this are done. I usually wind up doing this instead of being the way I want. Perhaps on day I will step from behind the table and out onto the dance floor, and to hell with what I should do. I'll do what I want.

Age 21

Random Musings

Do you know me?

Do you know me?

I am the one who is thought to be intangible.

I am the one who is supposed to know how to be around you.

You, who doesn't tell me what you are looking for.

Do you know me?

I am the one who struggles to understand what you want.

I am the one who is calling to you.

Are you listening?

Will you answer?

Do you know me?

Well, if you don't, is that completely my fault?

Age 21

Random Musings

Observations

He is walking too briskly.

The dog in the yard pursued him, but his barking was drowned out by a passing bus.

Crickets screech throughout.

A branch falls from a tree.

A car squeals to a stop as the low rumble of cars is increasing.

Vague chatter can be overheard from a group of girls across the street.

Packs of cars pass by in spirits.

A car door slams. Another.

Another bus is heard.

Someone plays a stereo too loud.

Age 21

Random Musings
These Nights

I love these nights the best. Cool, crisp air, the air even smells clean, fresh. I close my eyes and my imagination takes over...

We open all the windows, start a fire. Soft jazz drifts from the stereo speakers. The crackling fire is heard faintly. Sitting, talking, as the fire slowly dies. Once it retires, so do we. The house is cooled by the gentle breeze. I slip into the bed besides him; my head on his chest, my arm draped over him. He gathers me up into his arms. He strokes my hair; his embrace gets tighter. I love these kinds of nights. I feel as if nothing could harm me. I am safe. Safe in his arms. Safe in knowing he will still be here in the morning.

I was feeling so much. I've never had known that. Can you miss what you've never known?

Age 21

Random Musings

The Mysterious Invitation

I received an invitation a couple of days ago from whom I could not tell because there was no return address. With a sense of precaution, I opened the envelope. It was a letter form of an invitation inviting me to some sort of party at the address of a house that I was sure was abandoned years ago. With extreme doubts, I finally decided to go and try to figure out what was going on.

I reach the house and use enough if was abandoned and practically rotted away. The wood shutters were corroded and falling off. All plant life around was either dying or already dead. No sign of life was not found. At the sight of this I should have returned to my car and drive off, but this nagging voice kept wanting me to investigate further, so I did.

I gathered enough courage to approach the door and without any force at all, gently knocked on the door. I do not know who or what I was expecting to answer

my knock, but I tried once more and with this try the door creaked open. I went inside no knows what lurked within. I entered what I believed was some sort of formal room; one meant for private gatherings or parties. It was a darkened room; a musky odor seemed to hang in the air. I walked into a wall of webs that hung from the ceiling. The dense air had a stench of death; of things gone rotten and decayed. A quick survey of the room and I noticed the chandelier was coated with cobwebs which dangled down.

The only light that was able to shine through was gray with dust. The only reason any light penetrated the gloomy surroundings was the mere fact that there were rips and tears in the thick purple velvet curtains. All the while I searched the room for some signs of life. I had that nagging feeling I was being watched. It was as if the room itself was upset with my presence, that I was disturbing it.

I could not make out the design on the wallpaper, if one was there to make out, because of the darkness. All that I could make out was the places were the paper was peeling off the wall. As I studied the wall, the noise of squealing rats within them seemed to become louder. Along the walls was bits and pieces of tattered antique furniture sets – an old couch mix-matched with an old musky chair and so forth. I took a step closer to investigate the furniture when I noticed how loudly the floor creaked. It seemed with every step I took, the more the room seemed to bemoan its displeasure at me. I finally decided to leave. As I headed for the door, it felt as if the room was glad that I was leaving, a sigh of relief is you will. The darkness was starting to drive me insane and I had to get out into the clean air and int the sunlight. I reached for the glass knob of the front door I didn't remember closing, but because of its age, it crumbled within my hand, and I became trapped, locked within.

Age 21

Random Musings

Shades of Light and Dark

Tis an odd feeling I feel. It is hard to describe, no wait, perhaps not. It is not hard to describe; in fact, there are too many ways to describe it that I become confused. I always experience the same feeling when we're nearby. It is an emotion, but who's to say which one. It is one of anticipation – like a young child on Christmas morn; one of warmth, like the warmth of the sun on a beautiful autumn day; one of joy, like when you come home and are greeted by your puppy with a lick on the nose; and one of fear, feat that every time we say goodbye, tis the last. That is when confusion sets in. If am afraid of goodbyes, why do I say goodbye every time we part? Why does he? Is that all I fear, him leaving or me being alone? Am I afraid that he has become so important in my life I could not deal without him? Or is it just the mere fact that I may have fallen in love and are afraid that he does not love me?

But the last is an improbability. I would know when I were to fall in love, planned or unplanned,

wouldn't I? How could someone know? How come I do not know? How could I ask that question to myself and not know? I realize now that I am not afraid of him, nor have any of the answers to the questions I continue to ask myself, but tis the emotion itself, confusion, that indeed frightens me. That emotion that falls between the shades of light and dark.

Age 21

Random Musings
The Child Within

Where did they all go? The dolls and the toy soldiers we used to play with when we were kids. Just stop and think of those jacks that disappeared over the years. How many water pistols and yo-yos do you remember throwing away? Or does it go along with one of those lines your parents fed you after they got rid of them – they must have grown legs and walked away. If we were gullible enough to believe half of what we were told, why didn't we go out and try to catch these walking toys? Maybe these toys of our past are still there, where we left them, lying under that tree in the yard or there in that dusty old chest in the attic, or they could have been quietly and carefully placed in a box in the corner of our minds so that they child within can continue to play.

Age 21

Random Musings

Ever have one of those days?

Don't own an oven,

don't' have any rope,

tried to OD,

but I ran out of dope!

Opened a vein,

And I thought it was mine,

So I guess they won't ask me to

Play twister next time!

Decided to jump off a skyscraper,

I left a suicide note,

But it was Thanksgiving Day,

And landed on a float.

Put a gun my mouth,

I could have sworn it was real,

But the flag popped out

And I puked my last meal.

Swallowed some poison,

I thought I was a goner,

But my hair fell out

And now look like Sinead O'Conner.

Age 22

Random Musings

We're Just Like a Love Song

We're just like a love song,

you and me.

We started out simple,

just like a melody.

Bust as the days passed

and our love reached new heights,

the band started playing

new sounds in the nights.

With every "I love you"

the bells sound clear

and echo with beauty

both far and near.

With every promise

of eternal devotion,

the band strikes up

in magical motion.

Trumpets flare

with every touch

when our eyes meet

and say so much.

Drums burst

into rhythmic sound

whenever our hearts

begin to pound.

From a passing glance

for a meaningful gaze.

Dreams strike up

in a musical blaze.

With every smile,

with every sign

violins

begin to cry.

A song so sweet

a song so real

Together forever we walk along

writing and living our wonderful song

Until the day comes

when we can no longer write

the beautiful music

that sounds in the night.

Until one last note

that our hearts are sending

fades into

our happy ending.

Age 22

Random Musings

Is it in the cards?

I never felt more intimidated than I do right now.

I am like a small child in a museum, or worse yet, an antiques shop looking at my surroundings in awe, and yet terrified to touch a single item.

I am not sure that it is only intimidation I feel.

Perhaps it is intimidation mixed with secrecy.

Why is it not known to anyone I am here?

Is it out of embarrassment? Fear? Or is it just that my existence is just not meant to be acknowledged?

Why such secrecy?

Is it my background? My lifestyle? Am I lacking something?

I feel I have to prove myself in order to be recognized.

Even though I sort through much doubt, I find myself not wanting to leave my present position.

Kathleen Lopez

It comes down to 'at least I have here', wherever here is.

But then again, did I really have here, and if so, is it enough?

Age 22

Random Musings

Muddled

A woman sits upon her couch.

As she runs her hand across the plush cushions,

She glares at the typewriter and at the stack of blank papers before her.

BLANK.

Writer's block.

Frustrated she decides to pace.

Every idea she has come up with was met with a huff, crumpled up, and tossed out.

She lights a cigarette, then remembers she's trying to quit and lets it burn in the ashtray.

Frazzled, she gulps down another cup of coffee.

How, she wonders, is she going to make deadline?

A cool ocean breeze blows through the apartment, refreshing her and her ideas.

Like a flash she sprints to her typewriter and begins to type-the block is broken.

Age 22

Random Musings

Wilderness

Miles of miles of trees.

Animals running free.

Just miles of miles of emptiness.

That is all that is left of me.

Drained of all my energy

of all my dreams to be.

Just miles of miles of emptiness.

That is all that is left of me.

Construction crews and machines

just come and go as they please.

Just miles of miles of emptiness.

That is all that is left of me.

Kathleen Lopez

I am a lonely tree.

I stand alone.

A forest which once stood

Was once my home.

A hotel now stands

where trees should be.

Just miles of miles of emptiness.

That is all that is left of me.

Age 22

Random Musings

Confusion

To speak when there are no words.

To be afraid of something you know not if it is there.

To reflect when there is nothing to look back upon.

To remember memories that you have yet to create.

To talk and yet say nothing at all.

To laugh and yet die of fright.

To hate but look back upon with fondness.

To swing and yet remain motionless.

To run when you cannot walk.

To understand completely and yet be utterly confused.

Age 22

Random Musings

You're

You're pastina and meatloaf

You're cigars and pipes

You're a Knicks game at the garden and Dodgers vs the Mets at Shea

You're *Rock me Amadeus* and *They're coming to take me away*

You're your Yankees cap

You're Homer and Sparky,

You're the Blue Duster, the Chevrolet, and the Cutlet

You're overnight grocery store food stocking

You're a blue portable eight track player and Beatles eight-track tapes

You're Archie comics

You're Star Trek and Star Wars, but mostly Star Trek

You're cursing on the Belt Parkway

You're drives out to Kings Plaza, the Island, and Rockaway Beach

You're complaining about going to see the tree but getting a hot dog from the vendor

You're Uncle Car

You're hitting up Nathans and getting cheese fries with those red sticks

You're mustaches and beards

You're wire frame sunglasses

You're bagels from *Deli on the Bay* and Knishes from *Shatkins*

You're having a CB in the car, talking to Pepper and the Blue Nun

You're walks over to Al Mitchel's place

You're bringing our dog Ginger home sitting in the inside pocket of your jean jacket

You're printing labels for everything in your office

You're putting a permanent basketball hoop up besides the driveway

You're gone now, daddy

And I miss you

Age 51

Random Musings

Afterword

Man, I haven't written a poem since my 20s. Life got in the way and honestly didn't feel moved to do so in some time. *You're*, well, that was stuck in my head for a year; the year since he passed. I only had bits and pieces of it. They would hit me at random times and out of nowhere really. Honestly, the one line that got stuck in my head, so much so that it had to be the first line was 'you're pastina' of all things. He used to cook me pastina. And no one could ever match his meat loaf, and none of us know why.

This is really just a listing of the things I associated with dad. Random flashes of memories. Some won't make a lick of sense to anyone, but it's all the things that made up my dad.

Random Musings

Visit my website and sign up for my newsletter, find out where I will be for my next signing, and how/where to order my books:
www.wordsmithpublishingllc.com

Be sure to follow me on my social media sites:
www.facebook.com/KatAndSyd
@wordsmithpub (TT and IG)

Releases available in eBook, Paperback, Hardcover, and Audiobook:

The Shuller Series
Between the Shades of Light and Dark
Prodigal Son
Sweet Child of Mine
Thirteen for Dinner

The Crawford Chronicles
The Calling Card Murders
The Symbolist
Bad Things Come in Threes

Anthologies
Untethered Threads
The Gathering
The Ho Ho Murders

www.ingramcontent.com/pod-product-compliance
Lightning Source LLC
Chambersburg PA
CBHW060336050426
42449CB00011B/2776